Exploring Our Baylands

By Diane R. Conradson

Published by San Francisco Bay Wildlife Society

Acknowledgements

"No man is an island, entire of itself." The words of poet John Donne are often used to describe ecological dependencies. They can also be used to describe an author's dependence on the expertise of his or her friends, colleagues and acquaintances. For their help in making this book possible, I am grateful to former professor H. Thomas Harvey, Professor of Biology at San Jose State University and pioneer in marsh ecology and restoration, now, alas, deceased; Lyman Fancher, who shared his knowledge about harbor seals; photographers Crayton Thorup, Ken Gardiner, Mike Boylan and others, whose exquisite images of salt marshes and marsh wildlife grace many of these pages; and to Linda Knoll, whose design brought all of the elements of this book together.

I am indebted to a number of experts, each of whom reviewed individual chapters. Phyllis Faber, Editor of the California Native Plant Society journal *Fremontia*; Ned Lyke, Professor of Biology at California State University, Hayward; Richard Orsi, Professor of History at California State University, Hayward; and Michael Rigney, Director of Coyote Creek Riparian Station. Each read and commented on appropriate sections of the book.

Funding for this book came from the U.S. Fish and Wildlife Service, as part of its ongoing effort to make salt marshes better known to all of us, and from Chevron Corporation and New United Motor Manufacturing, Inc. Additional funding came from donations in the memory of Robert Stirrat. This book is published by San Francisco Bay Wildlife Society, a nonprofit organization that assists the education programs of the U.S. Fish and Wildlife Service.

Refuges and reserves are the results of the time and efforts of many people. To all of them, we owe our gratitude.

Diane R. Conradson

Introduction

Ducklings hatch and migrating waterfowl flock here, flying over bird watchers and autumn hunters alike.

To many people rushing down the freeways, the salt marshes and mud flats bordering San Francisco Bay are a dismal-looking wasteland. But for those people curious enough to walk through the marshes, the "wasteland" is a place of quiet beauty and open space, a community of plants marvelously adapted to flourish in salt lands, a home to dozens of different animals, and a wayside rest to millions of migrating birds.

Bayland sanctuaries preserve remnants of San Francisco Bay as it existed 200 years ago. Here are places where fish spawn in shallow waters, to the delight of anglers. Strange marsh plants excite the botanists. Ducklings hatch and migrating waterfowl flock here, flying over bird watchers and autumn

hunters alike. For the ecologists, the entire Baylands community is a dramatic example of the interaction of organisms with their environment. Most of all, these sanctuaries are time machines where people can turn their backs on the fast-paced complexities of human endeavors and face the slowly evolving ones of nature.

A marsh, like all of nature's creations, is a dynamic system: always changing, never static. With the passage of time, bodies of water tend to fill in and are converted to land; a marsh is a halfway point between water and land. Plants growing in shallow waters trap sediments and organic material which winter streams and summer tidal waters bring in. The plants themselves die and add to the fill. Gradually, more marshland is created.

The baylands of 200 years ago formed a vast community of nearly 800 square miles of mud flats, salt marshes and shallow waters.

An undisturbed salt marsh evolves in the same way, slowly shifting the intertidal zone Bayward. One series of plants and animals replaces another as the marsh builds itself higher and drier on the landward side and expands into the mud flats. Other forces such as scouring currents and waves, violent floods, drought, elevation changes and human activities easily hasten or reverse this process, for a salt marsh is a fragile system, precisely balanced.

The baylands of 200 years ago formed a vast community of nearly 800 square miles of mud flats, salt marshes and shallow waters. It still contains one of the richest assemblages of plants and animals of any natural community in the world. In the shallow tidal areas all the "seafood" lives — clams, mussels, oysters, crabs, shrimp, scallops, worms and the young of many fish. These feed the waterbirds and shorebirds that migrate, winter, or reside here permanently, sheltered by the low marsh plants. The salt marsh plants purify the air, and the Bay's salty waters help to clean out sediments and pollutants deposited in the Bay.

As the Baylands and Bay waters shrink because of human efforts to make more "land," an irreplaceable fragment of nature is being lost. Now, after people have exploited the Bay for

When the Bay itself was first explored in 1775, the Spanish sailors saw even greater expanses of marshes around San Pablo and Suisun Bays.

two centuries, they are beginning to recognize the San Francisco Bay estuary as the greatest natural resource in the Bay Area.

When Captain Rivera climbed a hill overlooking the Santa Clara Valley in 1769, becoming the first European to look upon San Francisco Bay, he saw salt marshes covering most of the south end of the Bay and rimming each side to Oakland and San Francisco. When the Bay itself was first explored in 1775, the Spanish sailors saw even greater expanses of marshes around San Pablo and Suisun Bays. How the men must have marveled at the shellfish, the salmon, the seals and sea otters, and especially the countless numbers of birds.

San Francisco Bay, as we know it, has been in existence for only a few thousand years. When some of our ancestors were painting cave walls in France with their exquisite art, there was no Bay, nor were humans present to watch it evolve. How then did our landscape come about? The answer involves an active earth, changing climates and living things that cannot always keep pace.

The Baylands Environment

D uring the past million years, San Francisco Bay has gone through four cycles of change from a great valley to a flooded estuary. During the last ice age, when much of the earth's water remained frozen in great glaciers instead of flowing back into the oceans, the sea level was at least 300 feet lower than it is today. The Bay Area coastline lay west of the Farallon Islands. Point Reyes and Devil's Slide were many miles from the shore.

When the last ice age began to end about 15,000 years ago, now-extinct species of horses, camels and ground sloths grazed on the floor of the present South Bay. As the glaciers melted, the low-lying land was covered by the rising ocean. By 10,000 years ago, an arm of the sea just reached the Golden Gate. Drowning of the land continued until about 5,000 years ago, when glaciers had melted to about their present size.

During the 10,000-year period of rapidly rising sea level, San Francisco Bay widened as much as 100 feet a year and deepened about eight inches every ten years. Five thousand years ago, the Pacific Ocean washed against a coast that lay only a few hundred yards west of today's beaches and cliffs. Most of San Pablo Bay had formed, and Suisun Bay and the Delta were being inundated.

Deepening of the Bay is continuing, but for the past five or six thousand years the rate has been only two-thirds of an inch every ten years. The main reason is not the rising sea level, however. The South Bay and Santa Clara Valley, which lie roughly between the Hayward and San Andreas faults, are slowly sinking while the surrounding hills are slowly rising. Fossil oyster beds of recent origin have been lifted well above sea level in San Pablo Bay. On the other hand, Bolinas, Tomales and Drakes Bays were all valleys that drowned as earth move-

Exploring Our Baylands

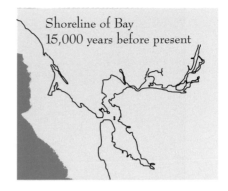

Shoreline of Bay
15,000 years before present

10,000 years before present

ments caused their mouths to subside into the ocean.

Evidence of human settlements left by ancestors of the Ohlone Indians dates back about 4,000 years. But recent archaeological findings indicate that humans may have reached the Bay Area 10,000 years ago. Perhaps their settlements lie on the old valley floor under two or three hundred feet of sediments and water.

When the sea level stopped its rapid rising, sand, silts and clay sediments, eroded from both the Sierra Nevada and the landscape surrounding the Bay, accumulated fast enough to balance the submergence in the Delta and North Bay. Salt marshes, which until then had formed only a narrow, discontinuous fringe in these areas, began to expand.

South Bay salt marshes, however, began forming only about 2,000 years ago. Two factors probably were responsible for the 4,000 year lag: first, the Santa Clara Valley end of the Bay was deeper; second, because it lay out of the mainstream of the sediment-laden Sacramento-San Joaquin River system, it received less eroded material needed to raise the substrate, or Bay bottom, to the tidal level where marsh plants could grow.

In the early 1850s, when the first American government surveys were made, tidal marshes were probably at their greatest expanse, covering about 313 square miles. Since then, about 12 percent of the Bay waters and 80 percent of the salt marshes

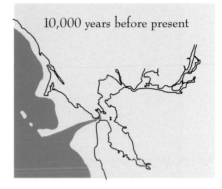

5,000 years before present

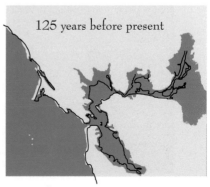

125 years before present

The Baylands Environment

Exploring Our Baylands

have been filled or diked in order to increase the amount of "useful" land. Suisun and San Pablo Bays were drastically shallowed between 1853 and 1884 as a result of hydraulic gold mining in the Sierran foothills. Tremendous quantities of sediments were washed into the streams and carried into the Delta and upper bays, where they were deposited in the quiet waters. The courts finally stopped this type of mining after waterways and agricultural lands became severely damaged. But its effects are still continuing. Over a billion cubic yards of mining debris filled in the watercourses between 1849 and 1914. Sediments eroded since then have been deposited mainly in northern San Francisco Bay because the bays upstream are "filled up." As a result of erosional and deliberate filling between the mean and high tide levels, nearly half of the present 60 square miles of tidal marshes have come into existence since 1850.

Because of the flow from the Sacramento River and the complex shape of the Bay, tidal water tends to flood in quickly and ebb out slowly in the South Bay, whereas the reverse is true in the northern reaches. The water spreads over the nearly flat marshes, then drains into a network of sloughs that return it to the Bay. Sloughs draining marshes that existed before 1850 meander in slow curves, while sloughs of the rapidly developed, post-1850 marshes trend straight across the marsh to the mud flats.

Tidal salt marshes start one to two feet below the mean tide level; water coming across them is usually quiet and shallow and has lost much of its force. Plants further slow the movement of the water, causing it to drop its load of sediments and thus build the marsh higher and farther into the Bay. Strong currents and waves may undercut the slough banks and drop blocks of marsh plants onto the mud flats as well as erode the Bay edge into a steep drop. A developing marsh, then, has a gentle slope while an eroding one, like many of those in the South Bay, ends precipitously.

Regardless of the slope, all tidal salt marshes have four zones, easily recognizable by what lives there. The low tide zone includes the mud flats with mats of algae; the midtide zone is characterized by stands of cordgrass; the high tide zone is covered with pickleweed; and the uplands marsh, farthest from the open bay, is where gumplant and salt grass flourish.

Circulation of Bay waters, with their loads of mineral sediments and organic particles, is complex and different in each part of the Bay. The water forms well-defined horizontal lay-

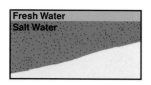

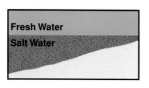

The denser salt water intrudes farther inland when the quantity of the lighter fresh water is reduced.

ers, with the denser salt water lying below the lighter fresh water. The two layers often move in opposite directions, with the sea water flowing in while the Bay water is still ebbing out. Since the overall water level remains relatively constant, the "thicker" the layer of freshwater flow from streams and rivers, the "thinner" the layer of salt water underneath it. By reducing the amount of salt water flooding up into the Delta and ends of the Bay, the freshwater layer prevents salt water intrusion up into the groundwater supply and the plant root zone.

The extremes of temperature and salinity to which Baylands life must be adapted occur in late summer and late winter. During summer, salinity can increase to three times its winter concentration until parts of South Bay are saltier than the ocean. Water temperature can increase 18°F from winter to summer. The exposed mudflats become even warmer and saltier than does the water.

The Bay receives about 80 percent of its fresh water and sediments from the Sacramento River during winter and spring. Even this amount represents only about half the historic outflow, the remainder having been diverted to the Central Valley and Southern California. Water from the Delta takes about two to three weeks to reach the Golden Gate in winter. It is held back mainly because the twice-daily tidal currents bring so much ocean water into the Bay that even winter floods and spring runoff cannot flow quickly out through the Gate. With less freshwater flow in summer, the time period is about two months.

The first major winter flow of water from the Delta can flush the water in the South Bay in one or two weeks, but by the end of winter, flushing takes a few months. By the end of the summer dry season, the South Bay takes five months to flush, since the water exchange is then controlled by tidal currents and wind mixing rather than by freshwater flow. The high temperatures and salt concentrations and low oxygen levels reduce decomposition below what the Bay can handle efficiently. With sewage and cannery wastes added to the natural particles in the water, the South Bay by the end of summer can become a very thick soup indeed.

With the water level, salinity, and temperature ranging so widely from day to day and season to season, it's a wonder that anything can survive in the Baylands. Yet San Francisco Bay Estuary continues to host a thriving variety of plants and animals.

Exploring Our Baylands

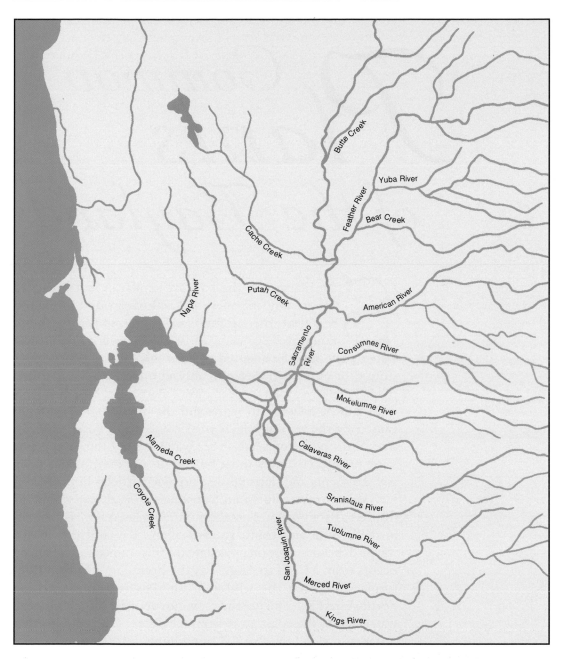

Freshwater system for the San Francisco Bay.

Common Plants of the Baylands

S alt marshes in the bay are similar in some ways to desert saline marshes such as those around the Salton Sea. First, there is little fresh water, so the water and the soil are very salty. Most plants cannot tolerate salt water; they must be adapted to keep salt out of their system, store it or excrete it. Second, although temperatures around the Bay are lower than those in most desert areas, Bayland plants must still be adapted to withstand the physiological drought caused by the drying effects of salt water and wind. Finally, since most of the minerals in sea water are not the ones plants need for growth, they must be able to obtain minerals from soil sediments and decomposed organic particles in the water.

Winter rains and spring snowmelt wash down sediments from San Pablo Bay and northern San Francisco Bay. But plants in the central and south reaches of the Bay and the coastal waters depend mainly on upwelling for their minerals. Upwelling occurs from March to August as the prevailing winds in California shift from the winter southerlies to the dry season northwesterlies. The northwest winds actually blow the ocean waters along the coast away from the shore. The cold bottom water rises to fill the "void," bringing with it the mineral-rich sediments that have accumulated on the sea floor. Strong spring tidal currents carry the minerals into the Bay where they fertilize the springtime algae bloom. Before 1850, the salt marshes were extensive enough to produce a quarter to half of the plant growth of the Bay; now algae in the water supply about twenty times as much plant material as the salt marshes.

As the land form slowly changed, some plants were forced out of "normal" environments, losing in competition to more vigorous plants. Those that were already adapted to tolerate salty conditions survived. Such plants are called **halophytes**. In a salt marsh, many halophytes must also be adapted to being regularly submerged by the tidal waters. Around the mean high tide level, where the submergence time is shortest, the soil in the marsh is usually the most salty. The salt content can fluctuate considerably with winter rain that washes out the salt, and evaporation during summer and fall that concentrates the salt. It is the yearly average of salt rather than the seasonal changes that helps determine what grows where.

The precise place in the salt marsh where each species of plant grows is determined by many interrelated factors, especially the amount of salt in the soil and the length of time of submergence. Because the amount of both salt and submergence time is directly related to the tidal level, plants tend to grow in distinct zones, or bands, parallel to the shoreline.

Plants are also zoned also by the average amount of fresh water they receive from streams and rivers. Salt inhibits growth in most plants. This becomes particularly apparent as one approaches Suisun Bay from the Golden Gate, since about 90 percent of the Bay's yearly supply of fresh water comes through the Delta to Suisun Bay. Salt marsh halophytes, which can tolerate salt concentrations greater than that of sea water, give way to salt-tolerant species of tules and cattails that grow in brackish water (water with a salt content between that of ocean

High Tide — — — — — — — —

Mid Tide — — — — — — — —

Low Tide — — — — — — — — —

High Tide — — — — — — — —

Mid Tide — — — — — — — —

Low Tide — — — — — — — —

water, 3.5 percent, and fresh water, less than 0.2 percent). These, in turn, are replaced by fresh water species where the salt level falls below .5 percent. The boundaries between salt, brackish, and freshwater marshes change as drought years alternate with high rainfall years, and salt water extends farther upstream or down.

The plants of the intertidal zone that fringes San Francisco Bay and the coastal bays are rarely affected by yearly rainfall variation since they are already tolerant of large seasonal changes in the salt content of water and soil. But water covering them at high tide is so turbid, or opaque, with silt and particles of decaying material that sunlight often cannot penetrate more than a few inches into the water. The rooted plants, the plants of the salt marsh, cannot grow much below the mean tidal level, the point where they are exposed to air about half the time and to enough sunlight to be able to photosynthesize sufficiently to survive.

Between the low tide line and the lower edge of the salt marsh lie the mud flats, rainwashed during winter and evaporated dry during summer. At low tide, they may extend several miles out into the Bay. The protected mud flats are often colored golden brown by a thin layer of one-celled diatoms lying on the surface. Leaflike sheets of sea lettuce, a thin, bright-green marine alga which tolerates changing salinity, lie on the mud or are washed into the marsh. Finely branching mats of green algal "scum" are found lying on rocks and mud flats or floating freely in protected waters. Most seaweeds grow only along the coast or just inside the Golden Gate, where the salinity remains close to that of the ocean and where they can attach to rocks, wood or other permanent surfaces.

Cordgrass is the only salt marsh plant able to tolerate many hours of continuous submergence, and it dominates the mid-tide zone. In late winter, the new grass growth may be totally submerged more than half the time, and in darkness for several days in succession if high tide occurs near mid-day. By summer, the dark-green grass is three or four feet high and topped with plumes of golden flowers held well above all but the highest tides. In places where the cordgrass is so thick that the plants are interlaced, wind and tidal currents may push down a few plants, which in turn pull down many neighboring ones, until large patches of grass are as flattened as if something had rolled over them.

To complete the yearly cycle of these perennials, cordgrass leaves and stems die back in the fall, coloring the mid-tide zone as tawny yellow as the dry hillsides encircling the Bay. Almost all the dried grass decomposes into minute particles full of nourishment, part of the "soup" for the microscopic animals, the filter-feeders, the detritus, or "waste," feeders, and the young of larger animals in the Bay.

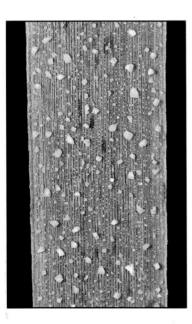

The white film on the cordgrass leaves is excreted salt crystals

Cordgrass is one of the most productive land plants in the world, yielding up to eight tons of dried material per acre. Productivity is usually measured by the amount of carbon converted from carbon dioxide into new plant tissue per year. Sugarcane and a few other agricultural crops are more productive, but they require extensive energy input from fertilizers, machinery and human labor. Cordgrass grows unaided by human manipulations, taking up carbon dioxide and even some carbon monoxide from the air and then releasing oxygen, helping to purify the air above the freeways that surround the Baylands.

When sediments become trapped in protected areas and along man-made jetties and levees, they may raise the level of the mud flats to the elevation where marshes can become established. Cordgrass is the pioneering plant of the salt marshes where sediments have been deposited up to a foot or so below mean tidal level. Seeds or pieces of roots broken from established plants float in the Bay until they become stuck in the mud and can begin to grow and spread. In laboratory experiments, cordgrass grows better in fresh water than in salt water. However, under natural conditions in brackish to freshwater marshes, cordgrass loses out in competition with the taller, only slightly salt-tolerant **tules** and **cattails**, with **alkali bulrush** in the drier middle marsh, and with other species of tules and cattails in the low marsh. It is forced to remain in the saltier environment where tules are not physiologically equipped to grow.

Most land plants lose fluids to salt water; they dehydrate, or "pickle." Halophytes, on the other hand, use part of their energy to take in salt water through their roots against an osmotic pressure gradient, filter out the salt, and excrete it through special cells in their leaves. The plants utilize the "fresh" water that remains. The higher the internal concentration of salt that the halophyte can tolerate, the less the difference in the

Exploring Our Baylands

osmotic pressure gradient between the inside and outside fluids and the less energy the plant needs to use to take in salt water. Hence, the "fresh" water may be much saltier than in "normal" plants. These adaptations are lacking in freshwater plants, eliminating them from a salty environment.

The conditions necessary for the seeds of salt marsh plants to germinate reveal their freshwater origin. Cordgrass seeds germinate best if they are soaked in cool salt water and then leached, or washed free of salt, in the fresh water of winter rains and runoff. Pickleweed seeds germinate best in mud leached almost free of salt, although the mature plants tolerate up to eight percent salt in the soil.

Pickleweed is the dominant plant of the average high-tide level, growing about 18 inches tall. Although it tolerates having its roots in wet mud, it cannot tolerate long periods of submergence. The cordgrass and pickleweed zones overlap for about three feet of elevation, with the cordgrass giving way as its environment becomes saltier and less frequently submerged. Competition is reduced in the overlap area because the cordgrass roots extend many inches below those of pickleweed. A typical emergent plant, cordgrass has spongy or hollow stems that bring air down to the root tips. Some of the air passes out of the roots, aerating the soil and possibly aiding the pickleweed to survive in the soggy mid-tide level. Pickleweed is often found in brackish water marshes, growing at a higher elevation than tules and bulrushes, which out-compete it in its lower range.

Pickleweed branches resemble a string of half-inch-long, gray-green pickles. The plant was originally believed to be leafless, photosynthesizing through its succulent stems like a smooth, spineless cactus. However, the "stems" are actually fleshy leaves, each "pickle" being a pair of leaves fused together into a short cylinder; the "string" running through the center

Pickleweed in bloom.

Dodder on pickleweed

of the leaves is the actual stem. The leaves do not excrete salt but store it, dissolved in water, in vacuoles, or little cavities, in cells at the ends of the branches. In fall, the leaves turn red, then dry up and decompose to enrich the Bay. Most species of pickleweed are perennials, sprouting again from the winter-dormant roots. Some people gather spring sprouts of pickleweed to cook and eat like asparagus, but by late summer, the leaves taste like concentrated brine. Tiny greenish-yellow flowers appear on the ends of the pickleweed branches in summer, with the male and female flowers being on separate plants.

The small, white blossoms apparently growing on pickleweed amid a tangle of orange threads are the flowers of a parasitic plant called **salt marsh dodder.** The seed of dodder germinates to form a rooted plant that grows until it reaches a branch of its host. Then the dodder develops the orange "threads," or stems, that send "roots" into the pickleweed. The rooted part dies and the dodder subsequently obtains all its food and water from the pickleweed. When its host dries up in the fall, the dodder dies, leaving its seeds to germinate in spring. Like most parasites, which must live in balance with their hosts so that both may survive, the dodder rarely kills the pickleweed. It may weaken its host, however, so that the pickleweed is less successful in reproducing or withstanding additional environmental stress. Other species of dodder grow on other host plants, with poison oak being a particular victim in the Bay Area.

Jaumea is another salt marsh plant so succulent that it is easily confused with pickleweed, especially where the two overlap above the mean high tide zone. Jaumea is rarely abundant, however, growing only in scattered patches through the high

Exploring Our Baylands

Salt grass

marsh. Its inch-long fleshy leaves grow from thick stems that are topped by yellow, dandelion like flowers. Many plants that grow in salty soil are succulent, for the more salt they take in, the more water they take in, until their leaves and stems become thick and juicy. Foot-high spikes of **arrow-grass** protrude through pickleweed in some marshes. Its narrow, basal leaves are hidden among other plants, but its stalks are covered with tiny white flowers in spring.

Above the upper boundary of pickleweed, runners of **salt grass**, resembling Bermuda grass, lay a dark green carpet on the mud. The same species grows around desert alkaline ponds and even around the sodium carbonate springs at Alum Rock Park in San Jose. In the same zone, **marsh rosemary** (sometimes called sea statice or sea lavender) flowers, sending up large, broad leaves and sprays of papery lavender flowers. **Alkali heath** spreads low mounds of small, curled-under leaves and pink flowers from the high marsh to the dry, salty uplands.

Numerous species of halophytes grow in the uppermost level of the intertidal zone where the highest tides wet the soil only a few times each year. The change of an inch or two in elevation changes the salt, water and oxygen concentrations, thus creating different environments to which different species are adapted. Most of the plants are under two feet high, giving a flat look to the landscape unless their flowers or fall leaves provide patches of color.

The saltbush family, well represented in the higher marshes, is easily identified by its leaves, which usually have grayish backs covered with tiny, white salt granules. **Fat hen's** dark green leaves are arrow-shaped and turn red in the fall. **Beets** and

Swiss chard, both garden escapees originally, have thick leathery leaves in response to the salty soil. Gray mats of **Australian saltbush** are common along all bays. This saltbush was imported from Australia to be grown in the high salt marshes as cattle fodder. Only in late summer and fall is it noticed, when its tiny red fruits show through its small leaves, and clouds of pigmy blue butterflies flutter above it. Most native insects cannot use introduced plants for food, since they lack the enzymes necessary to break down the different chemicals present in new plants. But the caterpillars of these tiny butterflies thrive on Australian saltbush.

Marsh grindelia or

gumplant

Many members of the saltbush family are "weeds," tough, hardy plants with numerous seeds, and tolerant of both alkaline and salty soil. **Russian thistle**, a saltbush tumbleweed, shares the upland area with **curly dock**, whose three- to four-foot high, red-brown stalk is prominent among the dry winter weeds.

In addition to jaumea, the ubiquitous composite, or daisy, family contributes **brass buttons**, a low succulent native to South Africa. Its small, bright yellow flowers resemble daisy centers without the white petals and often give vivid color to patches of high marsh. **Marsh grindelia** or **gum plant** grows at a slightly higher and drier elevation, forming a straggly bush with numerous two-inch, yellow, daisylike flowers that are in bloom most of the year.

Brass buttons

In brackish water marshes, diked off from the daily tides but subject to salt water seepage and freshwater flooding, tules grow in standing water about mid- tide elevation. Cattails replace them in the shallower water. Alkali bulrush grows in the middle marsh at the high tide level, leaving pickleweed to grow around and above it, often higher in elevation than pickleweed would normally grow in a tidal marsh. Above that, the upland weeds take over.

Because salty soil and submergence place such severe limits on plants, there are only about 15 native species and a few introduced ones adapted to living in the tidal salt marshes around San Francisco Bay. About 30 native species live in the

Exploring Our Baylands

more brackish water of San Pablo bay, with the number increasing to 80 in the Delta.

Above the elevation reached by even the highest tides, the salt marsh gives way to dry uplands or, along streams, to brackish-to-freshwater tule and cattail marshes. Because the soil is salty and salt water lies only a few feet below the ground, deep-rooted plants do not grow well. Hence, the dry uplands often contain many introduced weeds that pioneer disturbed areas. These salty but dry grasslands support animals such as meadow mice, jackrabbits and meadowlarks, species usually found in open fields.

The salt marshes are a low and monotonous wasteland to many people. But nowhere else in the Bay Area is one able to see and feel so much space and solitude as in the vast stretches of marshlands.

Common Invertebrates
of the Baylands

Crab

The Bay waters abound with tiny predators, most of which are themselves eaten – a hierarchy of eaters and larger eaters until a heron, a harbor seal, or a human feasts. Energy stored and ready to be eaten – bacteria, phytoplankton (microscopic diatoms and dinoflagellates) and detritus (fragments of decomposing plants and animals) feed the zooplankton (copepods, rotifers and larvae of larger organisms). Except for the tiny fish, the zooplankton are all invertebrates, and most are consumed by other invertebrates such mussels, barnacles and worms.

The Baylands has a variety of habitats: wooden pilings, rock and concrete breakwaters, sand, mud flats, salt marshes, salt ponds, salt water and brackish water, quiet pools and swift currents. Each has its own specific inhabitants. Most aquatic invertebrates have a free-swimming larval stage, no matter how little mobility the adult may have. Scientists believe that the adult animals may give off chemicals that the young sense in the water and follow back to the adults. Thus, the young can locate and settle down in their appropriate environments.

The Bay's native invertebrate species are relatively few in number, perhaps because the great San Francisco Bay estuary is so new geologically that only a relatively few species from previously existing bays have reached it during the past 10,000 years. About a hundred marine invertebrate species have been introduced, either accidentally or deliberately, since 1850, with nearly two-thirds of them coming from the Atlantic coast. These exotic animals (biologists call any non-native species "exotic")

Exploring Our Baylands

established themselves in the Bay and either out-competed or eliminated the native animals, since the natural controls – predators, diseases and competitors – were rarely brought along with the introduced species.

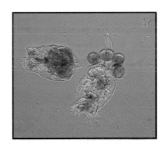

A barely visible rotifer carrying her eggs.

Most of the introduced fouling, boring and ballast-dwelling animals came on ships. Although a few were brought in as early as 1775, a multitude of new species arrived on ships bringing the gold seekers of the 1850s. New species continued to be inadvertently introduced, many of them now coming from the Orient, the South Pacific and Australia.

A later influx occurred with the completion of the transcontinental railroad in 1869. **Atlantic oysters** were sent overland by train and are still raised commercially at Point Reyes and Tomales Bay. They were followed by **Pacific oysters** from Japan in the early 1900s. These large oysters never did thrive within the Bay, perhaps because oysters are very sensitive to any kind of pollution. But their companions thrived. A single oyster shell may have on it dozens of species of other animals. With the mud, algae and water pockets mixed with the oysters packed for shipment, the oyster culture business has spread more marine animals around the world than any other agency. Dozens of Atlantic and Japanese invertebrates have become naturalized in San Francisco Bay ever since growers chose to raise larger oysters rather than the tastier, smaller, native **Olympia oysters**. Even the seaweed in which Maine lobsters are packed for shipping brought in another Atlantic snail during the 1960s.

A cyclop-eyed copepod with her egg case.

In 1986 another mollusk made its appearance, having jour-

Mud crab found on muddy banks and under stones on bay shores.

neyed as a microscopic larva from Asia, probably in the ballast water of a cargo ship. The **Asian clam** is now one of the dominant invertebrates of the Bay, numbering as many as 2,000 individuals per square foot of mud.

Nearly one-third of the introduced animals are crustaceans, a group which includes shrimp and crabs. The introduced species are usually small and sometimes destructive, many of them isopods and amphipods – pill bugs and beach fleas. One species of **pill bug** that arrived from Australia in the late 1800s burrows into the banks of sloughs and dikes, often weakening them until they collapse. Barely visible crustaceans called **copepods**, many with a single ruby-red eye, are a major food source for small fishes and filter feeders such as clams.

Several species of small, native **bay shrimp** and the **Oriental shrimp**, accidentally introduced about 1954, live in either deep or intertidal waters. Although a delicacy, especially in Shrimp Louis salads, their major value is as bait and as an important food source for fishes, since they are usually too small for humans to shell for food.

Native **mud crabs** scavenge through the cordgrass and live in burrows in the mud. Native **hermit crabs** often live in the shells of the introduced **mud snails** and **oyster drills**. At mid-tide levels in the sandier areas, the pink **ghost shrimp** lives in burrows with the opening on top of low, conical hills. At the low-tide level in the mud flats lives its relative, the grayish-colored **blue mud shrimp**.

Brine shrimp

The strangest crustacean of the Baylands is the reddish-colored **brine shrimp**, which can live in brine that varies in salt concentration from less than that in sea water to 30 percent salt! Brine shrimp feed on a reddish-colored alga, *Dunaliella,* which grows only in concentrated salt water, also up to 30 percent salt. The alga contains a red pigment that masks the green of its chlorophyll. Hence, many salt ponds are red-colored from both the algae and the brine shrimp. The low-salt concentrate green ponds are colored green by algae that are also eaten by brine shrimp.

Brine shrimp, like all fairy shrimp, are beautifully adapted to live in temporary ponds which remain dry for years. The small, reddish eggs of the brine shrimp must become com-

26

pletely dry and then return to the water before they will hatch. Sometimes the dikes around the salt ponds are covered inches deep with eggs that look like fine, red sand. Because the eggs stay viable for many years, they are collected commercially and packaged for fish food.

Over 20 percent of the exotics are mollusks – snails and bivalves, or two-shelled animals. The native Olympia oyster, once so numerous that cement manufacturers harvested their shell beds for lime, still exists in small numbers where pollution has not wiped it out. The mud flats and gravelly areas are home to the native **littleneck, bent-nosed** and **Baltic macoma clams**, and to several introduced species, including the **soft-shell** and **Japanese littleneck clams**, both so abundant that they are potentially harvestable. The introduced species have largely displaced the native clams. Other extremely abundant introduced clams, the quarter-inch long **gem clam** and the inch long **Asian clam** are too small to be of use to humans, but have become very important food for the Baylands birds.

Only three mollusks are usually visible to the observer. The native **bay mussel**, which attaches to permanent surfaces such as rocks or pilings, was harvested, along with the native oysters and clams, by the Ohlone Indians. The introduced **horse** or **ribbed mussel** of the South Bay protrudes out of the mud flats just below the mid-tide level. Mussels secrete byssal hairs, or threads, that bind them to one another in a mat. The mat holds the mussels in place on the mud and also helps prevent the mud from eroding. Mussels are filter feeders, siphoning in the Bay water and straining out the edible particles. Their phosphate-rich wastes are concentrated into tiny pellets and voided back into the Bay. The feces can then remain available as food for detritus feeders, such as the worms, or be deposited in the mud and fertilize the plants, rather than washing out into the ocean.

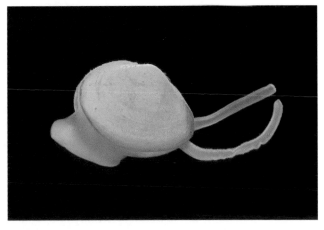

Always visible at low tide are hundreds of introduced **mud snails**, looking like dark pebbles scattered thickly over the mud flats. They crawl slowly about in the shallow water, feeding on diatoms

Baltic macoma clam

Mud snails crowd the mud flats.

Horn snails

that they scrape off the mud with their rasping tongues. On the mud flats they compete successfully for food and space with the long, slender **California horn snails**, a favorite food of the Ohlones. They are also known to eat the juvenile horn snails, which may account for the disappearance of the native snails from many mud flats along the Bay. Introduced **oyster drills** prey on many species of native and exotic mollusks.

The mud flats and muddy Bay bottom are home to numerous species of worms. A few crawl on the mud or swim,

Exploring Our Baylands

but most are sedentary tube builders, usually burrowed in the mud. The big **lugworm** typifies the detritus-feeding habit of many burrowing animals. It swallows mud and sand, digests out the organic material, and passes the mineral sediments through its body, defecating them in long, coiled, earthworm-like castings. A **clam worm**, *Neanthes*, introduced with the Atlantic oysters, lives in sandy mud and is an aggressive predator on bottom dwellers such as clams. A giant relative of the clam worm, sometimes reaching five feet in length, builds a tube in the sandy mud and swims in the waters of Elkhorn Slough.

Because there were so few native species in the San Francisco estuary, and indeed in most of the geographically isolated estuaries along the Pacific coast, many of the introduced species have no native competition. However the native animals have probably been reduced in numbers where competitors have come in, particularly the few species adapted to live in brackish water. The addition of hard-surfaced, man-made structures in the Bay has added new habitats for animals that must be permanently attached. The Bay is still a place open to pioneering!

The salt marsh shelters a large number of insects, especially flies, beetles and wasps. But these actually eat only a very small fraction of the living plants, with almost all the plant tissue decaying into food for the filter and detritus feeders. Close inspection of quiet pools and salt ponds should turn up salt marsh species of **water boatmen, mosquitoes** and **flies.** Halophytes growing above the pickleweed zone and both the dry upland weeds and brackish-marsh plants are food for myriad butterflies – introduced white **cabbage butterflies,** yellow and black **anise swallowtails,** orange **west coast ladies,** yellow **sulphurs** and brown **buckeyes.** The smallest butterfly in North America, the

Western pygmy blue butterfly

western pygmy blue with its half-inch wingspan, feeds on salt marsh saltbushes. Like the small animals of the Bay waters and mud, the small animals of the ground and air are food for the larger creatures, usually the birds and mammals.

Common Vertebrates
of the Baylands

As the tidal waters flow over the mudflats and salt marsh, small fishes swim with the tide to search for worms, clams, shrimp, and the still smaller fish that feed on the plankton, or microscopic animals and plants. Shore anglers catch **topsmelt, shiner, surfperch**, and **staghorn sculpin** while the fishes are foraging in the shallow water. Pipefish swim vertically among the water plants, looking like very thin versions of their close relative, the sea horse. During winter, **Pacific herring** spawn along the shores of Richardson Bay. **Striped bass, northern anchovy, sturgeon**, and many bottom fish such as the **starry flounder** depend on the shallow waters for food or places to spawn. **Chinook salmon**, which once spawned in almost every tributary of the

Stag-horned sculpin

Jackrabbit

Sacramento and San Joaquin Rivers, still navigate through the Bay. Low tide may expose depressions in the mud about 18 inches deep and several feet to yards long. These have been made by **bat rays** digging for soft-shell clams and other mollusks.

Nearly 60 species of fishes require the deeper water — salt, brackish or fresh — to complete their life cycle. All the fishes are ultimately dependent upon the detritus of the marshes and algae of the water to feed the creatures that feed them.

Some vertebrates are conspicuous because of their absence. Although the croaking and splashing of frogs is often heard in the upland freshwater marshes, no amphibians live in the dehydrating environment of the Baylands. While **gopher snakes** and **fence lizards** may search for food in the highest tidal zone, the reptiles, too, do not tolerate the salt.

Several mammals live in the Baylands, and numerous species visit the marshes at low tide to search for food. **Striped skunks** prowl the marshes for insects or bird eggs. **Raccoons** walk across the exposed mud flats looking for any seafood tidbits they can catch. **Gray foxes** hunt for seafood as well as mice and other small vertebrates. **Opossums** eat anything edible. Dogs and cats menace the wildlife even if they are not hunting for food. Recently, new predators have appeared in the Baylands. Non-native **red foxes** range far into the marsh where they eat endangered California clapper rails and their eggs as well as ducks and shorebirds.

The **black-tailed hare**, or **jackrabbit**, crosses the dry grasslands to nibble on saltbush and juicy pickleweed. If its long ears pick up any noises or its eyes catch any sudden movements, its long, powerful hind legs send it leaping and zigzagging across the marshlands to safety. Where dense dry land growth borders the marsh, the small **brush rabbit** may venture a few feet into the upper halophytes. When danger approaches, it darts under the cover and remains motionless rather than running away. The **beechey,** or **California, ground squirrel** lives in burrows in the dry grasslands above the marshes and also in the levees, where its extensive excavations can cause them to collapse.

Several native rodents live in the salt marshes. The **California vole**, or **meadow mouse**, is found in almost any moist meadow from sea level to mountain tops. The higher salt marshes and grasslands are criss-crossed with the animal's neatly trimmed runways, for its life often depends on a quick means of escape. Meadow mice, which have several large litters a year, form a major part of the diet of many Baylands predators, including hawks, owls, herons and gulls.

The grasslands above the marshes are home to the **western harvest mouse**, which is also at home throughout most of California and the west from the seacoast to the high mountains. The **salt marsh harvest mouse** is found nowhere in the world except in the salt marshes in the Bay Area. As the rising sea level isolated the mouse populations thousands of years ago, it evolved into two distinct subspecies, one living around San Francisco Bay and the other around San Pablo and Suisun Bays. Both subspecies may have evolved from populations of western harvest mice that were tolerant of a salty environment. These mice, if they continue to survive, offer scientists an opportunity to study organisms in the process of actually evolving into separate species.

Both species of harvest mice are nocturnal, and therefore rarely seen. The salt marsh harvest mouse feeds mainly on pickleweed and other marsh plants and seeds. It can drink the brackish Bay water directly, as well as satisfy its thirst with dew, rainwater and the fluids in succulent plants. Efficient kidneys rather than special glands rid its body of salt.

The upper pickleweed marsh is the salt marsh species preferred habitat. But when the highest tides drive it out, the mouse moves to the grasslands bordering the marsh. Often these have been filled in or otherwise destroyed, leaving the

Salt marsh harvest mouse, the red-bellied subspecies of the South Bay.

animal exposed to its predators. The salt marsh harvest mouse cannot exist where either the pickleweed or the uppermost edges of the salt marshes have been destroyed.

With its survival totally dependent on the survival of salt marshes fringing the Bay, the little salt marsh harvest mouse is considered an endangered species by both the federal and state governments. As with most endangered animals, the destruction of its particular habitat for more economically valuable uses, rather than outright killing by humans, is bringing the salt marsh harvest mouse to the finality of extinction.

With its cool wind and watery expanse, the Baylands hardly appears desertlike. But the adaptations of many salt marsh plants and animals, such as those of the salt marsh harvest mouse, are similar to those of desert dwellers which also must cope with the drying effects of salt.

Vagrant shrew

The **vagrant shrew** lives on wet ground under abundant cover. It can sometimes be seen on the mud flats at low tide or on the levees at very high tide. It is the smallest mammal of the Baylands; in fact, shrews are the smallest mammals in the world. Although it resembles a small house mouse, the shrew is a ferocious predator. It feeds ravenously on any animal it can capture, although its usual diet is insects. Its metabolic rate, the rate at which it utilizes food and oxygen, is one of the highest known for any mammal. A shrew must eat almost continuously day and night, or it will die of starvation in a few hours.

Sewage plants, dumps, buildings, and other sites of human debris attract the foot-long **Norway rat**, the smaller **black rat,** and the **house mouse**, all of which came to California as stowaways on the earliest ships. These animals provide food for some of the larger birds, but they also compete successfully for food and space with the less aggressive native animals, and may harbor transmittable diseases.

Although the little mammals of the salt marsh are rarely seen, exceptionally high tides that occur about the beginning

Harbor seals

hauled out.

of each new season flood them out of their homes onto the tops of the highest plants, levees and piers. At these times, predatory birds such as hawks, gulls and herons easily capture and gorge on the helpless animals, a natural (although by human feelings, unpleasant) display of salt marsh relationships.

The largest Baylands mammal, the **harbor seal**, is usually found in protected sloughs and inlets, often hauled out and lying on the mud flats or marsh plants, always moving to keep close to the water's edge. Humping along like a giant caterpillar on land, the harbor seal is powerful and graceful in the water. It often swims in channels alongside boats, to the surprise of sailors who occasionally think they are being followed by a shark.

Unlike a sea lion, the harbor seal cannot bring its rear flippers forward, and therefore cannot easily climb onto higher rocks for protection while it rests. It is particularly wary and

Exploring Our Baylands

easily disturbed by human activity, whereas sea lions and elephant seals can tolerate humans walking through their rookeries even during the pupping season. When a harbor seal haulout site is repeatedly disturbed, the seals may abandon it permanently.

As many as 300 harbor seals still haul out in the San Francisco Bay National Wildlife Refuge near Newark from late March to early June to bear pups. Harbor seals form into groups, with individuals behaving independently rather than gathering in great colonies of dominant males and harems of females and pups. Dozens of pups are born at the Newark site each year. Pups are born at only two other sites in the Bay. They are weaned and live on their own only four to six weeks after birth. After the pups are weaned, most of the harbor seals move to one of the half dozen haul-out grounds within the Bay and around Point Reyes. Many protected coastal beaches and harbors south of the Golden Gate are also used for haulout grounds. A particularly good area from which to view the seals and their pups without disturbing them is along the cliffs at Point Lobos State Reserve south of Carmel.

The Ohlone Indians killed the seal for its fur and meat. Harbor seal bones, found at the bottom of Indian shell mounds in Coyote Hills Regional Park at Newark, are about 3,000 years old. No one knows how many seals lived in San Francisco Bay in 1800, but they were slaughtered in great numbers for their coarse fur until 1900, by which time the population was considerably reduced.

How long harbor seals will continue to haul out in the Bay, surrounded by over seven million people and their activities — especially when people become aware of their presence and want to view them at close range — really depends on how much the animals will be left alone. Increasingly, the same is true of the Baylands habitat and most of its inhabitants.

Birds
of the Baylands

The most exciting and aesthetic experience one can have in the Baylands is seeing thousands of birds, many of them standing or swimming or flying only a few yards from the viewer.

Although three dozen species of Baylands birds are permanent residents, the Pacific Flyway, the migratory sky route followed by millions of birds, brings in at least another 100 species. The flyway begins in the Arctic, and gradually collects more and more ducks, geese and other water birds and shorebirds from Alaska, western Canada and the United States as it courses south along the Pacific coast. When this "highway in the sky" reaches Tule Lake in northern California, a small number of birds continue their migration east of the Sierra Nevada. Most follow the coast. About 50 species spend the winter around San Francisco; others stop briefly to rest and feed before continuing their migration to southern California, Mexico, Central America and even southern South America. A few species, such as swallows, phalaropes, and most of the terns, are summer visitors that come north from South America.

The low, dense salt marsh vegetation shelters the Bay's birds from storms and predators. The water and mud flats, filled with worms, crustaceans, mollusks, fishes and little rodents, feed them. The tidal waters and soft mud discourage human intruders.

The primary restriction on the number of water and shorebirds appears to be the limited amount of mud flats and marshes along the Pacific coast rather than a lack of living space or food

Exploring Our Baylands

Snowy egret

in their spring or summer nesting areas. Like most natural populations, birds live at their biological maximum. Each bird must have its physical place in the world or die. As habitats are destroyed for other uses, their inhabitants cannot go elsewhere because "elsewhere" is already supporting its maximum population. Birds, like most animals, are largely creatures of instinct and would not go elsewhere anyway. The Pacific Flyway provides the water birds' pattern of life; the marshes and mud flats of the San Francisco Baylands provide their living space.

There are essentially three habitats for Baylands birds: marshes, mud flats, and open water. A few species take advantage of man-made salt ponds and levees. The marsh cordgrass and pickleweed shelter many birds that high tides may flush briefly into the open.

Among the wading birds, the largest is the **great blue heron**, four feet high with a seven foot wingspread. Its long legs and long, heavy bill allow it to stand in deeper water and catch larger fish than any other Baylands bird. In the fields and marshes, it catches insects and rodents, even large rats. With prey too large to swallow whole, the heron tosses the animal into the air, catches it sideways, then snaps its bill up and down the body to "tenderize" the animal before swallowing it head first. Birds usually do not spear through their prey; they lunge at it and catch it in their bill. If they spear it, they quickly push or shake it off. Great blue herons frequently fly to ponds and shallow lakes around the Bay to fish. One enterprising bird stalked the goldfish in the reflecting ponds at the IBM plant in

Birds of the Baylands

San Jose until it had eaten every fish.

For several unlucky great blue herons, their eyes were bigger than their throats. Two birds were found recently that had choked to death trying to swallow three-foot long lampreys, while others have been found with various species of oversized prey fatally wedged in their throats.

The **great egret**, a white heron over three feet high, slowly stalks through the shallow waters, marshes and fields, watching for fish, insects, and mice. Unlike the great egret with its yellow bill, the smaller **snowy egret** has a black bill. Standing about 18 inches high, it shuffles its feet through the mud and water of shallow ponds to stir up crustaceans and intertidal fishes.

The three herons frequently share a tidal pond where their different sizes and behaviors greatly reduce the competition among them. The great blue heron stands motionless waiting for prey to come to it; the great egret slowly stalks its food; and the snowy egret walks actively through the water to flush a tidbit. These herons also frequent open fields, farmlands and sheltered ocean coves, where they sometimes stand on the floating kelp and look as if they were walking on water.

From the 1870s until the early 1900s, when huge hats decorated with feathers or entire birds were the fashion for women, great and snowy egrets were mercilessly hunted for their beautiful, lacy mating plumes. During that period when a servant's wages were ten dollars a month, a hunter received five dollars for each bird skin. Both male and female birds were shot at the height of the courting and nesting season when their feathers were the most beautiful, often leaving fertile eggs and nestlings to die. The birds nearly disappeared from Florida and other

Great blue heron, great egret, snowy egret

Exploring Our Baylands

Snowy egrets fishing

southern states that have extensive marshes. Not a single great egret was reported in south San Francisco Bay from 1880 to 1928. The snowy egret was thought to be gone from all of California between 1900 and 1908.

The threatened loss of these two birds led to the formation of the National Audubon Society. As colony after colony was wiped out by plumage hunters, conservationists in Florida banded together to petition their legislature and the United States Congress to pass laws making it illegal to kill the birds or sell their feathers. A bird protection law was passed in 1901, but there were no funds to enforce it. In response, a group, which became the forerunner of the National Audubon Society, raised money to hire four wardens. In 1905, one warden was killed trying to protect the birds. Soon afterwards, poachers began to receive fines and jail sentences, fashions changed, and the traffic in feathers ceased. Very slowly the birds began to increase their range and numbers until today they are again a frequent and spectacular sight.

The **black-crowned night heron** usually remains inactive and well-hidden in the marsh vegetation until evening, when it begins to feed and call noisily. Being nocturnal, it has little competition from the other herons. A little larger than a snowy egret, but much chunkier, it appears to stand hunched over with its short neck pulled down on its back. The adult is pale gray with a black back and cap sporting a long white plume. The immature bird, brown with whitish stripes on the breast, resembles the American bittern, which is occasionally found in salt marshes.

Black-crowned night heron

Herons usually nest in large colonies, or rookeries, to which they return each year. They may build huge stick nests on top of redwood and eucalyptus trees, as they do at Audubon Canyon Ranch north of Stinson Beach, or on top of shrubs or even on the ground. Within San Francisco Bay, the Marin Islands near San Rafael and Bair Island near Redwood City have supported large heron rookeries. The colony on Bair Island, which once numbered several thousand nesting pairs of four heron and egret species, has been virtually abandoned because of heavy predation from the introduced red fox and the death of coyote brush nesting bushes. But herons and egrets will typically abandon a colony in favor of another area. One relatively new colony is located in tule marshes near the Don Edwards San Francisco Bay National Wildlife Refuge's Environmental Education Cen-

Exploring Our Baylands

ter in Alviso. It is likely that many of the birds that were forced to move from the Bair Island location found suitable nesting sites at the Alviso colony.

Surprisingly, although we have snowy egrets here all year, the birds that we see nesting at Alviso and the Marin Islands are not the same birds we see foraging in sloughs and bay mud flats during the winter. By banding young birds at the Bair Island colony during the late 1970's, scientists have determined that most of our breeding egrets spend the winter on the sunny shores of Southern California and northern Mexico. Where our wintering egrets come from is still a mystery.

Rails are secretive birds of salt and freshwater marshes, often difficult to find. Fifty years ago, the **California clapper rail** was fairly common in the tidal marshes of the Bay Area, but habitat destruction and hunters almost wiped it out. Today it is an endangered species, facing at least one new problem that is causing the biologists at Don Edwards San Francisco Bay National Wildlife Refuge, charged with protecting the remaining population, to literally stay awake nights. The latest problem for the clapper rails is a predator native to the midwestern United States — the red fox. By capturing and attaching radio transmitters to adult rails, refuge biologists have been able to track rails as they feed in the labyrinth of sloughs, and have found remains of rails at the mouths of red fox dens. In a desperate attempt to save the remaining rails, estimated in

A not-so-secretive clapper rail.

the early 1990s at between 300 and 500 birds, the refuge biologists have undertaken an extensive predator control program. They hope that this program will help insure the survival of this unique Baylands bird.

The **Virginia rail** and **sora** can be seen occasionally in the salt marshes when high tides drive them from shelter. The very rare, tiny **black rail** winters in the salt marshes. During a recent high tide, one was trampled to death when it ran into a group of people stalking through the marsh trying to see it.

In the same family as the rails is the always abundant **American coot**, or **mud hen**. A gregarious bird except when nesting, it grazes on tender grasses and other plants (young rice plants of the Delta are a special delicacy), feeding at the water's surface or diving to dine on underwater growth. The coot's feet complement its varied feeding habits. Huge lobed toes enable it to swim and dive as well as if it had webbed feet while also letting it walk on soft mud without sinking or sticking. Like many other birds that dive from the water's surface, the coot has to taxi across the water, flapping and paddling in order to gain enough speed to take off in flight. Most surface diving birds must have stretches of water for "runways," though they may nest in marshes.

Killdeer and nest.

Almost any well-watered grassy field is habitat for the **killdeer** — cemeteries, golf courses and farmlands as well as upland marshes and shorelines. Although other members of the plover family are long distance migrators, the killdeer is a common resident bird. The female lays pointed speckled eggs in a shallow hollow on gravelly ground. Young killdeer, like the young of most water and shorebirds, are precocial — eyes open, covered with down, and ready to follow their parents to shelter and food minutes after hatching. The killdeer parents protect the eggs and young from predators by one adult fluttering away from its offspring as if it had a

Exploring Our Baylands

broken wing, leading the "enemy" away, and then slipping quietly back to its brood.

The related **black-bellied plover** is common from fall through spring. In summer, it migrates between its breeding grounds on Arctic tundra and its wintering grounds, which range from the tidal marshes of the Bay Area to southern Brazil. Many of these foot-long birds migrate 20,000 miles a year!

The mud flats support the shorebirds in almost countless numbers. Ten thousand birds may feed along a thousand foot strip at the water's edge. We are only now beginning to understand just how important the mudflats, salt ponds and other wetland habitats are to these seemingly innumerable shorebirds. The Point Reyes Bird Observatory began an intensive volunteer-based survey of shorebird populations in 1988. During periods of peak migration in both the spring and the fall, shorebird numbers in San Francisco Bay may top 1,000,000! San Francisco Bay is probably the most important shorebird habitat in California.

Close as they may be to one another, the different species of birds on the mud flats are rarely competing. In the balance of nature, if two similar species compete for the same limited resources in the same place at the same time, one will eventually die out. Where different species of shorebirds feed together, their sizes, shapes, food tastes and behavior patterns result in their partitioning the resources, as is seen with the herons and egrets.

The depth of water first determines the spacing. The little **least sandpipers**, or **peeps**, feed in small flocks in the film of water left by the receding tide. Their sparrow-size bodies and short legs and bills are not adapted for deep wading or probing in the mud. Instead, they pick up small fly larvae, crustaceans and tiny worms on or just under the mud surface. Another peep, the slightly larger **western sandpiper**, is highly gregarious and probably the most common shorebird in the Bay Area during the fall and spring, with flocks numbering up to 50,000 individuals. Wading belly deep in two inches of water, they probe the mud, feeling for worms, small crustaceans and tiny mollusks such as gem clams. The sight of a large flock of Western sandpipers flying in unison, flashing first their white underparts, then their gray-brown backs as they turn and twinkle in the sunlight is a thrilling reward for any bird watcher.

The largest of the peeps are the **dunlins**. Though almost

Marbled godwit

never seen in summer, they are particularly common in mid-winter. Their size allows them to wade and probe a little deeper for larger bits of food than the western or least sandpipers feeding close by.

Also in the sandpiper family are several of the larger probing shorebirds. **Willets** are common resident birds along the coast as well as the Baylands, where their favorite food is mud crabs. The nondescript grayish-brown birds become spectacular when startled into flight. With loud, eerie cries, they rise on black wings striped with a broad white band. The startle effect may cause a predator to hesitate long enough to allow the willet to escape. When they land and fold their wings, the willets again become an almost invisible, dry, mud-colored lump, slowly walking on the flats or resting in the marsh.

Like the peeps, the **short-billed dowitcher** is a rapid prober. From fall through spring it is often found in large flocks mixing with the larger waders. Its straight bill and foot-long body distinguish it from the smaller sandpipers. The **long-billed dowitcher**, almost indistinguishable from the short-billed species, is usually found in freshwater marshes. The **greater yellowlegs** is a solitary bird, more slender than the willet, with bright yellow legs. From fall to spring it feeds in the ponds and pools, actively catching swimming animals by lunging at them rather than by probing. The **marbled godwit**, more distinctly marked in brown and beige than the other sandpipers, feeds near the water's edge with avocets and black-necked stilts. It plunges its entire head under water and probes with its four-inch long pinkish bill for any edible mud flat inhabitant. The most easily identified shorebird must be the **long-billed curlew**. Its total body length is about two feet, with a third of that length its down-curved bill! The curlew wades belly deep, plunging its head under water and its bill several inches down into the mud to feel for the deepest worms, clams and other burrowers.

All these members of the sandpiper family feed when the tide is receding, and rest during the high-tide periods, regardless of whether it is day or night. Thousands upon thousands

Exploring Our Baylands

of shorebirds appear on the mud flats as the tide ebbs, then disappear as it rises. The low marsh plants conceal them, causing the Baylands to look all but deserted. Many shorebirds wait out the changing tides on the levees surrounding the salt ponds, where they can see approaching enemies — and be seen — more easily.

Avocets, about the same size as the godwits, are easily recognized by their white body, and black and white back and wings. Since they are resident birds, bird watchers can enjoy the cinnamon-red head and neck feathers of their spring breeding plumage. The avocet's four-inch long bill is slender and upturned, hardly useful for probing in mud. Instead, this bird wades deep into the water on six-inch long legs and pecks at floating animals and seeds or sweeps the mud surface for food, often with its head completely under water. Laying its bill tip on the mud, it sweeps its head sideways searching for small invertebrates. Many shorebirds taste/feel for animal life with sensory receptors near the end of their bill tip. In addition, the avocet's partially webbed toes allow it to swim when the water becomes too deep for wading. Then it feeds like a dabbling duck — head down, tail up.

The closely related **black-necked stilt** nibbles on insects in the marshes and picks brine shrimp from the salt ponds. About half as heavy as the avocets, the active, agile stilt must bend its seven-inch-long, bright pink legs deeply in order for its bill to reach the ground.

Avocets waiting for the tide to turn

Both avocets and stilts have strange behavior patterns of extending and bobbing their heads and necks and flapping their wings in what were formerly believed to be courtship patterns. Now it is thought that these distraction displays, like those of the killdeer, are used to confuse predators, especially during nesting season, since both birds nest in the open on the tops of barren salt pond levees. If distraction by the adults does not deter predators, even the most acute vision would be almost useless in finding the perfectly camouflaged young which lie motionless, sometimes for hours, after being disturbed.

Stilt chick in the marsh underbrush.

The different feeding habits of the avocets, stilts, marbled godwits, and other birds reduce competition for the same invertebrates among these several species of birds feeding side by side. Their different leg lengths allow one kind of bird to wade deeper than another, even when the birds are about the same overall size. Actually, birds walk on their toes. The backward bending "knee" is the bird's ankle. The visible "leg" is the combined length of its foot and

Black-necked stilts.

lower leg, with the feathers replacing the scaly skin where the "calf muscle" begins. The actual knee is usually hidden among the belly feathers. Most shorebirds wade about ankle-deep into the water.

Intertidal ponds are often scattered through the salt marshes. As the twice daily tidal waters flood across marshes

Exploring Our Baylands

and fill the ponds, the small mud animals become active, moving about or exposing their siphons or tentacles. Then the dabbling, or pond, ducks come out of the vegetation to feed. Most common, especially in fall and winter, are the **mallards**, many of which become permanent residents, the elegant brown and white **pintails**, and the **northern shovelers** with their huge, shovel-shaped bills. During the breeding season, the most common species is the **gadwall**, which nests on islands and in the vegetated fringes of the Baylands.

Mallards are the ancestors of most domestic ducks. Even in the wild, they are less wary than many other species, and spend much of their time on land. White barnyard ducks have been bred from albino mallards. Like most albino animals, they are less aggressive and more easily tamed than normal-colored wild stock. Many domestic animals are white, bred to retain albinism and the gentle traits associated with it.

The beautifully colored male **cinnamon teal** is a frequent sight in winter, but **green-winged** and **blue-winged teals** are seen only occasionally. Most of the female ducks look alike to the casual viewer — drab brownish ducks. Since the males do not share in the nesting or rearing of

Northern shoveler

the young, they can flaunt their colors to attract mates, whereas the females are camouflaged to blend with the grassland and marsh plants.

Dabbling ducks rarely dive, but instead tip head down-tail up when feeding. Since they can feed only as deeply as they can reach aquatic plants and animals in this position, shallow water is essential for their survival. Most of the diving birds need take-off space according to their size. But surface-feeding dabbling ducks spring straight into the air from the water, so they are able to utilize the small, shallow marsh ponds. Although diving ducks are rarely found in salt water marshes, they often stay in protected shallow waters, diving to feed on mud flat species when the tidal waters flow in.

Sea ducks, such as the **surf** and **white-winged scoters**, which are often seen on the open Bay, may dive 40 feet deep for food. Others, such as **canvasback** ducks, will dive to the bottom in only a few feet of water as they follow the rising tides, although they dive in deeper water as well. San Francisco Bay is crucial for the survival of the Pacific Coast's canvasback population because well over half of the 90,000 canvasbacks that migrate along the Pacific Flyway winter here, particularly around San Pablo Bay. The remainder stop to feed and rest.

Mallard ducks

Western grebe.

The protected channels and coves are dotted in winter with small ducks that are black at both ends and pale gray in the middle. These are male **lesser scaups**, "bluebills" to the hunters, and they are usually accompanied by the dark-brown females. Tiny, rusty brown **ruddy ducks**, with their fan-like cocked tails, are resident birds. In spring, the male's breeding plumage is brick red.

The equally tiny **pied-billed grebe** is a resident bird of protected shallow waters, often diving quickly when disturbed only to pop up more than a minute later many feet away. In winter, flocks of **horned** and **eared grebes** rest and dive for fish in the salt ponds and shallow open waters. A few big **western grebes** gather in channels and the Bay, but most spend the winter near the kelp beds of the open ocean. Grebes, like a number of the deep-diving birds, have their legs set so far back on their bodies that they have difficulty walking. They build floating nests anchored to marsh plants and rarely come on land.

The wintering **white pelicans**, gliding on rising thermals or floating in shallow coves and salt ponds in the South Bay, often congregate in flocks numbering up to a thousand or more. They usually fish from the water's surface. **Brown pelicans**, most frequently seen in summer, plunge from the air to catch fish in the coastal waters or the open Bay.

Brown pelicans, common until 1969, have been consid-

Exploring Our Baylands

Brown pelican

ered an endangered species. Most scientists believe that the pesticide DDT accumulated in the birds through the food chain, interfering with their fertility and eggshell development. Recent studies have indicated that several additional factors may have contributed to the birds' decline, including other pollutants, disease, and especially stress from people disturbing them. As some of these problems are diminishing, the brown pelicans are slowly making a comeback, even to a small breeding population as far north as Point Lobos. An evolving problem may be a diminishing food supply as the temperature of the ocean along the coast appears to be rising enough to cause schools of fish to disappear.

Double-crested cormorants flap across the sky or swim in the channels, their long black necks giving them a snaky appearance. They are a startling sight roosting on the high-tension towers paralleling San Mateo Bridge or on levees along the Hayward shoreline. **Brandt's cormorants** are common on the open coast, breeding in great colonies on rocky ledges around Point Lobos and Point Reyes.

Cormorants, unlike most water birds, do not have sufficient oil in their feathers to keep them continually dry. As a result, the feathers become soggy after a prolonged stay in the water. The birds sink lower and lower until they are all but

Cormorants dry
their wings

submerged and can scarcely rise from the water. They then fly laboriously to an exposed perch to stand, wings outstretched, until their feathers dry. In the Orient, cormorants were used to catch fish. A ring attached to a long cord was slipped around each bird's neck to prevent it from swallowing the fish it caught. The birds were trained to give the fish to the owner and received a few as a reward after the ring was removed.

Aptly named "sea swallows," the graceful terns seem to patrol above the channels and sloughs, watching head down, ready to dive into the water for fish. Often mistaken for gulls, terns are smaller and much more agile in their flight, aerodynamically aided by a forked tail and narrow, pointed wings. Most of the terns winter in Central and South America, returning in the spring to breed in gregarious colonies.

The tiny **least tern** once nested on the sandy coastal beaches. Human developments destroyed its habitat, and human use of the beaches during spring disrupted its nesting cycle. With a population reduced to the endangered level, some least terns have begun to nest around the Bay on salt pond dikes, which are also the nesting sites for the big, scarlet-billed **Caspian terns** and the common **Forster's terns**. Unfortunately, these ground-nesting species are also vulnerable to predation from introduced predators such as Norway rats and red foxes. A number of least tern colonies scattered throughout San Francisco Bay have been either totally abandoned or the number of breeding pairs has been reduced substantially in the last ten years primarily due to increased predation.

Exploring Our Baylands

Least tern and chick

Gulls are the opportunists of the water birds' world. Garbage dumps, fishing sites and processing plants, plowed fields, any park, school yard or shopping center with food scraps, as well as bays and beaches attract them. **California, ring-billed, glaucous-winged**, and **herring gulls** scavenge for scraps any time of the year except during the nesting season. Then, in late spring, most of the gulls migrate north or east to nest around inland waters, from central California to the Rockies, Canada, or Alaska.

Although many Bayland bird species are facing difficulties, occasionally one species defies the trend. One such is the California gull. Ten years ago 95 percent of the state's California gulls bred in one location — Mono Lake near the California-Nevada border. Most of these gulls nested on islands in the lake, whose freshwater sources were being depleted by Southern California users faster than they could be replaced by winter snow or rain. The lake level was rapidly dropping. As a result of the lowering water level, one of the islands became a peninsula, allowing coyotes and other land predators access to the colony. In 1981, 97 percent of the California gulls' eggs and nestlings died or were killed by predators. Ninety five percent of the California gulls that breed in the state could have been lost. In addition, the lake water was apparently becoming too salty for algae, brine shrimp, and brine flies, the gulls' food, to survive.

In 1982, a small colony of California gulls began nesting on a salt pond island near Alviso. Since then, that colony has grown to over 4,000 birds. At the same time, legal battles to allow snow melt to replenish Mono Lake have been successful and the gull colonies at Mono Lake are again producing new generations of California gulls.

Tern-sized **Bonaparte's gulls** bob on the salt ponds in winter as they feed on brine shrimp and insects. The little gulls often remain long enough into summer to grow the striking black head feathers of their breeding plumage before they migrate to Alaska and Canada. The dark-gray, crimson-billed **Heermann's gulls** breed around the Gulf of California and summer on the open coast of the Bay Area. The only other locally nesting gull is the big, dark-mantled **western gull**, which is usually seen along the ocean nesting in spring atop sea stacks and island slopes. In San Francisco Bay, it nests on the Marin Islands and on Alcatraz.

Many species of gulls have a spot or ring near the tip of the bill contrasting with the bill's color. Newly-hatched hungry gulls know instinctively to peck at this spot when the parents bring food. The pecking action stimulates the parents to feed their young. Without this stimulation, the adults seem unable to release the food.

The Baylands are the breeding and feeding grounds for

Ring-billed gull

spectacular birds of prey. Gliding on its four-foot wing span just above the cordgrass blossoms, a **northern harrier** banks sharply, exposing its white rump patch, then twists down, perhaps to rise with a mouse or bird in its talons. Flocks of shorebirds rise frantically from the mud flats when this hawk flies overhead, then drop to hide in the sheltering plants. The smaller, falcon-like **white-tailed kite** hovers on rapidly beating wings over the upland marshes and grasslands as does the pigeon-sized **American kestrel**, hunting grasshoppers and mice. **Short-eared owls** nest in the upland marshes and hunt over the open fields, often during the daytime. The bays and open coast may have **ospreys** nesting on a tree snag or rocky pinnacle and fishing in quiet waters.

Many land birds find food and shelter in the salt marsh

Exploring Our Baylands

vegetation. The resident **song sparrows** spend their entire lifetime within an area of a few acres, rarely moving out of dense cover. As a result of their restricted movement, the birds have become isolated in the marshlands, possibly by a tolerance of or preadaption to the salty environment. The isolation has led to the evolution of several subspecies of salt marsh song sparrows, similar to the evolution of the salt marsh harvest mouse.

Northern harrier in flight

At low tide, **red-winged blackbirds** hide in the marsh along with flocks of **starlings**. **Marsh wrens** sing from the bulrushes, and an occasional flash of yellow identifies the **salt marsh yellowthroat**, a little marsh warbler. The same isolation mechanism which led to several distinct subspecies of song sparrows has also led to the evolution of a salt marsh race of the common yellowthroat. Unlike most of the other upland races of yellowthroats which breed in California, the salt marsh yellowthroat is nonmigratory, spending the winter along with song sparrows and marsh wrens within the fringes of the Baylands. In spring salt marsh yellowthroats move to freshwater marshes to breed. Because of continuing habitat destruction, particularly of freshwater breeding areas, this race of yellowthroat is a

Burrowing owl

Exploring Our Baylands

candidate species for endangered status.

House sparrows, house finches and **pigeons** look for seed and crumbs on the dry, peopled places. In the spring and summer, **barn** and **cliff swallows** scoop mud from the tidal ponds for their nests and catch insects on the wing. In the upland marshes and grasslands, **western meadowlarks** sing and **burrowing owls** peer at passersby from old ground squirrel burrows.

Many other water, shore, and land birds are permanent, seasonal, or transient residents of the Baylands. To all, this habitat extends the elements for survival — food, rest, and refuge.

Western meadowlark

In Parting

Environmental education
at San Francisco Bay
National Wildlife Refuge

This then is a salt marsh community and a few of its citizens. It and they are wholly dependent upon us for their continued existence. From the lacy egrets and the twinkling flocks of sandpipers to the delicate western pygmy blue butterflies, nothing can exist without the open acres of "dismal-looking wasteland" marshes, tidal mud flats and shallow waters of the Bay. Each "improved" acre leads a plant or animal one step closer to the dark oblivion of extinction.

When we severely limit the space left to natural populations we doom the remaining inhabitants to slow extermination. One pair or ten pairs or one hundred pairs of creatures do not necessarily mean that the species will continue to survive. Accidents, disease, lack of space for refuge , lack of food — these are not the only hazards. Too much inbreeding in a limited population often results in weaknesses fatal to the entire population. Some birds react to a kind of "mass psychology." They flock and migrate, court, nest and raise their young in response to the actions of the entire group. If the group is

Exploring Our Baylands

too small, the remaining members cease to perform the functions necessary to continue their existence.

At the National Audubon Society's 1962 convention, staff biologist Roland Clement summed up the present status of all living things:

South Bay tidal channel

"Man has suddenly become the chief determinant of organic evolution on this planet. Not only has culture been substituted for ordinary biological selection in our own case, but our remaking of the face of the earth to suit our every whim will soon decide what other species, if any, are to survive.

The species most threatened in our day are those whose habitats have been all but preempted by man...in almost every case (where a species is threatened by extinction) losses of habitat, whether by direct preemption or damaging alterations, were the cause of a decline which left remnant populations precariously dependent on great good luck in Nature's uneven course, and absolutely dependent upon the self-restraint of mankind."

The Bay has been exploited for its bounty ever since the first humans arrived on its shores thousands of years ago. The Ohlones of the South Bay and the Coast Miwoks along its northern reaches harvested the plants and animals for food, clothing, housing, tools and shell money, and traded the surpluses. The Indians had neither the technology nor the population numbers to affect the productivity of the Bay. At no time in its 4,000 year history did the entire Indian population of the greater Bay Area exceed 25,000 people. Since each small tribelet had its own territory averaging two people per square mile, no single area of the Baylands was exploited beyond recovery.

By 1776, seven years after first sighting the Bay, the Spanish had mapped it from the delta to the Golden Gate and designated the sites for the Presidio and the Mission Dolores. Thirty years later, the Russians entered the Bay, seeking trade with the Spanish. Within a few years, Russian settlements had been established at Fort Ross, Bodega Bay and on the Farallon Islands, and the sea otters had been nearly exterminated for their luxurious fur. Even the Hudson's Bay Company had an outpost at Yerba Buena.

The Mexicans held a tenuous grip on the Bay Area.

Andrew Jackson offered to buy San Francisco Bay for $3,500,000, but the negotiations fell through. Nonetheless, in 1846, the undaunted Americans raised their own flag over Yerba Buena, changed its name to San Francisco, and claimed the Bay just in time for the gold rush. Exploitation began in earnest.

The first Bay fill was in Yerba Buena Cove. Promoters dumped dirt even on the ships deserted by the gold seekers and over existing piers and shorelines, leaving former waterfront property far inland. Beginning in the 1860s, the shallows of San Pablo and the South Bay were diked off to create salt evaporation ponds. Today, about 55 square miles of former marshlands are covered with salt ponds. (Ninety percent of the water must evaporate in order for the salt to be commercially harvested, a process that takes five years to complete.)

On the intertidal mud flats, oyster farms were fenced off to keep out the predaceous skates and sea stars. (Human preda-

tors, author Jack London among them, would steal the oysters at low tide on foggy mornings.) About the time that the Atlantic and Pacific oyster industry failed in the early 1920s, beds of fossil oyster shells, up to 30 feet deep, began to be harvested for their lime content, which was used to make cement.

Soon after the gold rush, Italian fishermen began taking shrimp from the Bay bottom waters with drag nets. Twenty years later, the Chinese began operating shrimp camps. Fights between the two nationalities over fishing territories were frequent and often lethal.

Meanwhile, diking, draining and filling continued. The Bay waters were reduced by 55 square miles, from 476 to 421 square miles. The marshlands were reduced from over 300 square miles to less than 60. The Bay became a sewer, a garbage dump, and real estate. By 1965, plans for Bay fill, developed independently by individual cities and counties without

Family life at Drawbridge, now a ghost town in Don Edwards San Francisco Bay National Wildlife Refuge

Exploring Our Baylands

any coordination, would have had tens of thousands of acres of tidelands and shallow Bay waters filled. San Mateo County even proposed to fill 23 square miles of the Bay with a billion cubic yards of fill. The top third of San Bruno Mountain would have been the source of the dirt.

While "fill and develop" were the rallying cries of most planners during the 1960s, small groups of people were rallying to save the Bay. Two Palo Alto members of the Santa Clara Valley Audubon Society, Lucy Evans and Harriet Mundy, began a crusade to save the municipally owned Palo Alto Baylands from fill and development. They were joined by Dr. H. Thomas Harvey, a Professor of Biology at San Jose State University, a baylands ecologist and a pioneer in marsh restoration. Under this leadership, other conservationists joined in the battle with City Hall, armed with facts and figures to support their values. In 1965, the Palo Alto City Council voted to set aside over 1,000 acres of salt marsh, mud flats, and shallow waters as a wildlife preserve and to provide a Baylands Interpretive Center and staff. The communities of San Francisco Bay now had a model for the methods to both preserve the Baylands and utilize it.

In Berkeley, site of a proposed 4,000-acre fill, wives of three University of California professors, Mrs. Clark Kerr, Mrs. Donald McLaughlin and Mrs. Charles Gulick, met and organized the Save San Francisco Bay Association. Save-the-Bay stopped that fill plan. Continuing efforts of Save-the-Bay and other organizations resulted in the McAteer-Petris bill in 1965 that stopped piecemeal fill and led to the establishment of the San Francisco Bay Conservation and Development Commission. The BCDC now reviews and rules on all applications for Bay fill, after weighing the advantages of each development proposal with the advantages to the public welfare and the lack of adverse effects on the wildlife, scenic beauty and wholesomeness of the air, water and climate. Filling, abandoning or changing the use of a salt pond requires a permit from the BCDC. The permit will be given or denied on the basis of the Commission's regulations. Over a quarter of the Bay's 276 miles of shoreline are reserved for recreation. Unfortunately, agencies such as the BCDC and the California Coastal Commission have become political issues, threatened with extinction by legislators pressured by developers and industry.

A similar grassroots effort by conservationists led to the

creation of Don Edwards San Francisco Bay National Wildlife Refuge in 1972. The refuge will one day protect over 40,000 acres of marsh, mud flats, and shallow water areas in the South Bay. It provides opportunities for outdoor education and wildlife-oriented recreation. The creation of the Golden Gate National Recreation Area and similar areas resulted in additional acres of protected shoreline, improved public access to the Bay, and much-needed recreation and education programs.

As the threat of unrestricted Bay fill was diminished, another threat has taken over. The Bay and its inhabitants receive over one third of the fresh water that falls on California. As the state's population continues to increase and as agriculture requires more and more water, the demands for water, especially the water "wasted" as it flows out the Bay and into the Pacific Ocean, are reaching a "life or death" cry. Dry cotton fields and swimming pools, proposed industry and housing developments — highly visible human needs — take precedence over "possible effects" — salt water intrusion, declining estuarine productivity and fishery catches, and destruction of the intricate ecosystems of San Francisco Bay. Projects like the Peripheral Canal, filled with promises to protect the Bay, will continue to be proposed in efforts to divert "excess" fresh water from northern to southern California. Since almost nothing is presently known about the effects of diverting fresh water from the Bay (nor will the studies be completed for years) the promises might well be too little and too late.

During the span of the earth's history, San Francisco Bay has been in existence for less than the blink of an eye but it has been a source of wonder and livelihood to humans during their entire co-existence with the Bay. Padre Pedro Font, who accompanied Juan Bautista de Anza in 1776, wrote of his first sight of the Bay: "And there we saw a prodigy of nature." De Anza himself, in more pragmatic terms, chronicled: "The port of San Francisco is a marvel of nature, and might well be called the harbor of harbors." Sixty years later, Richard Henry Dana saw the Bay and predicted: "If California ever becomes a prosperous country, this bay will be the center of its prosperity."

Today, the Bay remains the heart of our prosperity. Its continued ecological health and habitation by all living organisms, including humans, are essential to that prosperity. Former Secretary of the Interior, Stewart Udall, summed up the significance of this prodigy of nature:

"The greatest single resource in this region is San Francisco Bay itself."

COMMON BAYLANDS PLANTS
cattail *(Typha* spp.*)*
salt grass *(Distichlis spicata)*
cordgrass *(Spartina foliosa)*
tule or bulrush *(Scirpus* spp.*)*
alkali bulrush *(Scirpus robustus)*
curly dock *(Rumex crispus)*
pickleweed *(Salicornia pacifica)*
Australian saltbush *(Atriplex semibaccata)*
fat hen *(Atriplex patula)*
quail bush *(Atriplex lentiformis)*
beet or Swiss chard *(Beta vulgaris)*
Russian thistle *(Salsola kali, S. soda)*
marsh rosemary, sea statice, or sea lavender *(Limonium californicum)*
alkali heath *(Frankenia grandifolia)*
salt marsh dodder *(Cuscuta salina)*
gum plant *(Grindelia humilis)*
Jaumea *(Jaumea carnosa)*
brass buttons *(Cotula coronopifolia)*
arrow-grass *(Triglochin* spp.*)*

COMMON BAYLANDS INVERTEBRATES
California horn snail *(Cerithidea californica)*
oyster drill *(Urosalpinx cinerea)*
mud snail *(Nassarius obsoletus)*
ribbed or horse mussel *(Ischadium demissum)*
bay mussel *(Mytilus edulis)*
Olympia oyster *(Ostrea lurida)*
Atlantic oyster *(Crassostrea virginica)*
Pacific oyster *(Crassostrea gigas)*
gem clam *(Gemma gemma)*
Japanese littleneck clam *(Tapes japonica)*
littleneck clam *(Protothacca staminea)*
soft-shell clam *(Mya arenaria)*
bent-nosed clam *(Macoma nasuta)*
Baltic clam *(Macoma balthica)*
Asian clam *(Potamocorbula amurensis)*
clam worm *(Neanthes virens succinea)*
giant clam worm *(Neanthes brandti)*
lugworm *(Arenicola brasiliensis)*
brine shrimp *(Artemia salina)*
burrowing pill bug *(Sphaeroma quoyanum)*

COMMON BAYLANDS INVERTEBRATES continued
oriental shrimp *(Palaemon macrodactylus)*
bay shrimp *(Crangon franciscorum, Crangon nigricauda,*
Crangon nigromaculata)
blue mud shrimp *(Upogebia pugettensis)*
ghost shrimp *(Callianassa californiensis)*
hermit crab *(Pagurus hirsutiusculus)*
mud crab *(Hermigrapsus oregonensis)*
Atlantic green crab *(Carcinus maenus)*
salt marsh water boatman *(Trichocorixa reticulata)*
salt marsh mosquito *(Aedes squamiger, A. dorsalis)*
salt marsh flies *(Family: Ephydridae)*
brine fly *(Ephydra riparia)*
western pygmy-blue butterfly *(Brephidium exile)*

COMMON BAYLANDS VERTEBRATES
bat ray *(Miliobatus californicus)*
white sturgeon *(Acipenser transmontanus)*
green sturgeon *(Acipenser medirostris)*
northern anchovy *(Engraulis mordax)*
Pacific herring *(Clupea harengus pallasi)*
king or chinook salmon *(Oncorhynchus tshawytscha)*
silver or coho salmon *(Oncorhynchus kisutch)*
bay pipefish *(Syngnathus griseo-lineatus)*
shiner surfperch *(Cymatogaster aggregata)*
staghorn sculpin *(Leptocottus aramatus)*
striped bass *(Morone saxatilis)*
topsmelt *(Atherinopsis affinis)*
starry flounder *(Platichthys stellatus)*
gopher snake *(Pituophis catenifer)*
fence lizard *(Sceloporus occidentalis)*
opossum *(Didelphis marsupialis)*
vagrant shrew *(Sorex vagrans)*
raccoon *(Procyon lotor)*
striped skunk *(Mephitis mephitis)*
gray fox *(Urocyon cinereoargenteus)*
red fox *(Vulpes vulpes)*
harbor seal *(Phoca vitulina)*
California ground squirrel *(Spermophilus beecheyi)*
western harvest mouse *(Reithrodontomys megalotis)*
salt marsh harvest mouse *(Reithrodontomys raviventris)*
    Suisun Bay subspecies *(R. r. halicoetes)*
    San Francisco Bay subspecies *(R. r. raviventris)*

COMMON BAYLANDS VERTEBRATES continued

California vole (meadow mouse) *(Microtus californicus)*
Norway rat *(Rattus norvegicus)*
black rat *(Rattus rattus)*
house mouse *(Mus musculus)*
black-tailed hare *(Lepus californicus)*
brush rabbit *(Sylvilagus bachmani)*

COMMON BAYLANDS BIRDS

(Including uplands marsh-grasslands species.)
horned grebe *(Podiceps auritus)*
eared grebe *(Podiceps nigricollis)*
western grebe *(Aechmophorus occidentalis)*
pied-billed grebe *(Podilymbus podiceps)*
white pelican *(Pelecanus erythrorhynchos)*
brown pelican *(Pelecanus occidentalis)*
double-crested cormorant *(Phalacrocorax auritus)*
Brandt's cormorant *(Phalacrocorax penicillatus)*
great blue heron *(Ardea herodias)*
great egret *(Casmerodius albus)*
snowy egret *(Egretta thula)*
black-crowned night heron *(Nycticorax nycticorax)*
American bittern *(Botaurus lentiginosus)*
mallard *(Anas platyrhynchos)*
pintail *(Anas acuta)*
green-winged teal *(Anas crecca)*
blue-winged teal *(Anas discors)*
cinnamon teal *(Anas cyanoptera)*
northern shoveler *(Anas clypeata)*
canvasback *(Aythya valisineria)*
lesser scaup *(Aythya affinis)*
white-winged scoter *(Melanitta deglandi)*
surf scoter *(Melanitta perspicillata)*
ruddy duck *(Oxyura jamaicensis)*
white-tailed kite *(Elanus leucurus)*
northern harrier *(Circus cyaneus)*
osprey *(Pandion haliaetus)*
kestrel (sparrow hawk) *(Falco sparverius)*
California clapper rail *(Rallus longirostris)*
Virginia rail *(Rallus limicola)*
sora *(Porzana carolina)*
black rail *(Laterallus jamaicensis)*

COMMON BAYLANDS BIRDS continued

American coot or mud hen *(Fulica americana)*
killdeer *(Charadrius vociferus)*
black-bellied plover *(Pluvialis squatarola)*
long-billed curlew *(Numenius americanus)*
marbled godwit *(Limosa fedoa)*
greater yellowlegs *(Tringa melanoleuca)*
willet *(Catoptrophorus semipalmatus)*
short-billed dowitcher *(Limnodromus griseus)*
long-billed dowitcher *(Limnodromus scolopaceus)*
western sandpiper *(Calidris mauri)*
least sandpiper *(Calidris minutilla)*
dunlin *(Calidris alpina)*
American avocet *(Recurvirostra americana)*
black-necked stilt *(Himantopus mexicanus)*
northern phalarope *(Lobipes lobatus)*
glaucous-winged gull *(Larus glaucescens)*
western gull *(Larus occidentalis)*
herring gull *(Larus argentatus)*
California gull *(Larus californicus)*
ring-billed gull *(Larus delawarensis)*
Bonaparte's gull *(Larus philadelphia)*
Heermann's gull *(Larus heermanni)*
Forster's tern *(Sterna forsteri)*
least tern *(Sterna albifrons)*
Caspian tern *(Sterna caspia)*
burrowing owl *(Athene cunicularia)*
short-eared owl *(Asio flammeus)*
barn swallow *(Hirundo rustica)*
cliff swallow *(Petrochelidon pyrrhonota)*
marsh wren *(Cistothorus palustris)*
starling *(Sturnus vulgaris)*
common yellowthroat *(Geothlypis trichas)*
house sparrow *(Passer domesticus)*
western meadowlark *(Sturnella neglecta)*
red-winged blackbird *(Agelaius pheoniceus)*
Brewer's blackbird *(Euphagus cyanocephalus)*
salt marsh song sparrow *(Melospiza melodia)*
    San Francisco Bay race *(M.m. pusillula)*
    San Pablo Bay race *(M.m. samuelis)*
    Suisun Bay race *(M.m. maxillaris)*

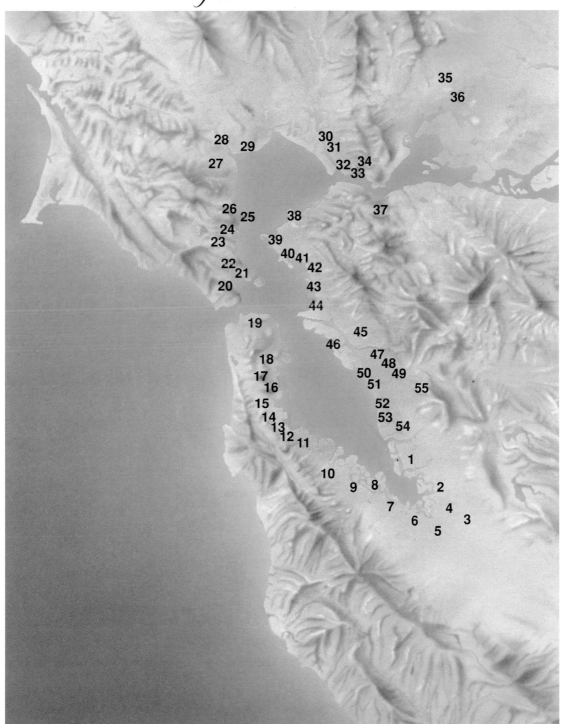

	Site	
1	Don Edwards San Francisco Bay NWR Visitor Center	Marshlands Road, Fremont
2	Coyote Creek Lagoon	Fremont Blvd., Fremont
3	Don Edwards San Francisco Bay NWR Environmental Education Center	Grand Blvd., Alviso
4	Alviso Marina	Hope Street, Alviso
5	Sunnyvale Baylands Park	Caribbean Dr., Sunnyvale
6	Mountain View Shoreline Park	Stierlin Road, Mountain View
7	Palo Alto Baylands Nature Preserve	Embarcadero Road, Palo Alto
8	Bayfront Park	Bayfront Expressway, Menlo Park
9	Port of Redwood City	Chesapeake Drive, Redwood City
10	San Mateo County Fishing Pier and Parks	Beachfront Blvd., Foster City
11	Coyote Point Park	Coyote Point Drive, Burlingame
12	Bayside Park	Airport Road, Burlingame
13	Burlingame Public Shore	Bayshore Highway, Burlingame
14	Burlingame Shorebird Sanctuary	Bayshore Highway, Burlingame
15	Bel Aire Island	North Airport Blvd., S. San Francisco
16	Oyster Point Park	Oyster Point Blvd., S. San Francisco
17	Sierra Point	Sierra Point Blvd., Brisbane
18	Candlestick Point	Gilman Ave., San Francisco
19	Golden Gate National Recreation Area	Various waterfront locations
20	Sausalito Waterfront	Bridgeway, Sausalito
21	Richardson Bay Park	Greenwood Cove Road, Tiburon
22	Richardson Bay Audubon Sanctuary	Greenwood Cove Road, Tiburon
23	San Rafael Shoreline Park	East Francisco Blvd., San Rafael
24	Loch Lomond Marina	Loch Lomond Drive, San Rafael
25	McNears Beach County Park	Point San Pedro Road, San Rafael
26	China Camp State Park	N. San Pedro Road, Santa Venetia
27	Petaluma River Public Fishing Access	Harbor Blvd., Black Point

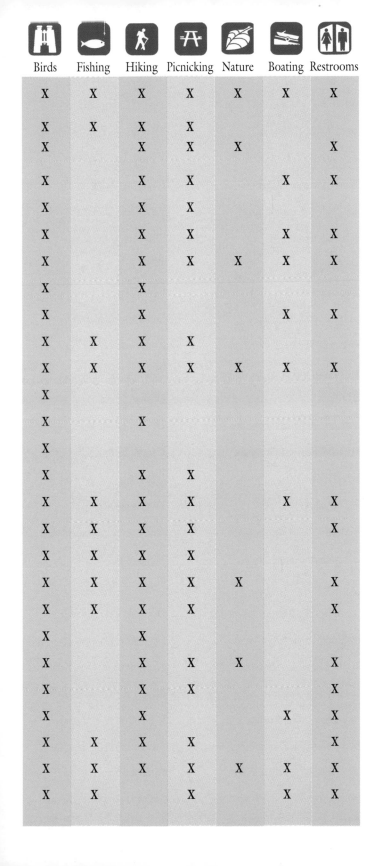

Birds	Fishing	Hiking	Picnicking	Nature	Boating	Restrooms
X	X	X	X	X	X	X
X	X	X	X			
X		X	X	X		X
X		X	X		X	X
X		X	X			
X		X	X		X	X
X		X	X	X	X	X
X		X				
X		X			X	X
X	X	X	X			
X	X	X	X	X	X	X
X						
X		X				
X						
X		X	X			
X	X	X	X		X	X
X	X	X	X			X
X	X	X	X			
X	X	X	X	X		X
X	X	X	X			X
X		X				
X		X	X	X		X
X		X	X			X
X		X			X	X
X	X	X	X			X
X	X	X	X	X	X	X
X	X	X			X	X

67

	Site	
28	Port Sonoma Marina	270 Sears Point Road, Sonoma Co.
29	San Pablo Bay NWR, Tubbs Island	Hwy. 37, Sonoma Co.
30	Vallejo Municipal Marina	Mare Island Way, Vallejo
31	Vallejo Parks	Wilson Ave., Vallejo
32	California Maritime Academy	California Academy Dr., Vallejo
33	Benicia State Recreation Area	Rose Drive, Benicia
34	Benicia Waterfront	First Street, Benicia
35	Suisun March	Kelley Street, Suisun City
36	Grizzly Island Wildlife Area	Grizzly Island Road, Solano Co.
37	Martinez Regional Shoreline	Ferry Street, Martinez
38	Point Pinole Regional Shoreline	Atlas Road/Giant Hwy., Pinole
39	Point Molate Beach	Point Molate Road, Richmond
40	Keller Beach	Dornan Drive, Point Richmond
41	Miller Knox Regional Shoreline	Dornan Drive, Point Richmond
42	Point Isabel Regional Shoreline	Central Avenue, El Cerrito
43	Berkeley Marina	University Ave., Berkeley
44	Emeryville Shoreline	Emeryville Marina
45	Lake Merritt, Lakeside Park	Bellevue Ave, Oakland
46	Crown Memorial State Beach	McKay Ave., Shoreline Dr., Alameda
47	Doolittle Beach	Doolittle Drive, Oakland
48	San Leandro Bay Regional Shoreline	Doolittle Drive, Oakland
49	Arrowhead Marsh	Swan Way, Oakland
50	Oyster Bay Regional Shoreline	Neptune Drive, San Leandro
51	San Leandro Marina	Marina Blvd., San Leandro
52	Hayward Regional Shoreline	W. Winton Ave., Hayward
53	Hayward Shoreline Interpretive Center	Breakwater Ave., Hayward
54	Coyote Hills Regional Park	Patterson Ranch Road, Fremont
55	Alameda Creek Regional Trail	Alameda Creek , Fremont

Birds	Fishing	Hiking	Picnicking	Nature	Boating	Restrooms
X			X		X	X
X		X	X			
X		X	X		X	
X	X	X	X			X
X		X	X			X
X	X	X	X		X	X
X	X	X				
X		X	X	X	X	X
X	X	X	X			X
X	X	X	X			X
X	X	X	X			X
X			X			X
X	X		X			
X	X	X	X			X
X	X	X	X			X
X	X	X	X	X		X
X						
X		X	X	X		X
X	X	X	X	X		X
X	X	X	X		X	X
X	X	X	X		X	X
X		X	X			
X	X	X	X			X
X	X		X			X
X	X	X				
X		X	X	X		X
X		X	X	X		X
X		X	X	X		